DISCOVERING WINGED INSECTS

Animal Book Age 8
Children's Animal Books

BABY PROFESSOR
EDUCATION KIDS

They fly! Some of them buzz! And sometimes they sting or bite! Winged insects are pretty amazing. Let's take a look at some.

MOST INSECTS ARE WINGED

Most species of insects can fly. For some species, like ants, only certain members of the colony develop their wings; and then they lose them when they don't need them any more. Other insect species, like dragonflies, spend most of their adult lives flying through the air.

Winged Ant

Black Fly

There are a few insect groups that used to be able to fly, but have evolved away from flying. And a very few insects like silverfish and jumping bristletails don't have anything to do with that flying stuff. All the other insects are happy to take to the air.

The other things insects have in common:

⇨ Their bodies have three parts: head, abdomen
and thorax
⇨ They have two antennae
⇨ They have three pairs of legs

Yellow Jacket Wasp

Spider

This makes them different from creatures like spiders, that have four pairs of legs and a body with only two parts. Find out about the differences in the Baby Professor book Insects and Arachnids. There are between six and ten million insect species in the world, too many to discuss in one book! So let's visit with just four of our flying neighbors.

HOUSE FLIES

House flies live almost everywhere that people live, except in Antarctica and maybe a few islands. They probably developed in Asia, but they like to live with people. So when people migrated to new areas, house flies went with them. If you go deep in the woods or up steep mountains to where there are no houses and people living in them, you will probably find no house flies unless you bring them with you!

House Fly

Flies in general first appeared over 250 million years ago, but house flies are much younger. The oldest house fly fossil found so far is from about 70 million years ago, at the end of the age of the dinosaurs.

House flies only live up to six days, even if you don't swat them. But the female is laying eggs through that whole time. They have lots of babies! When you hear the buzzing of a house fly, that's the sound of their wings. The wings beat as much as one thousand times every minute! However, they fly very slowly, less than five miles per hour.

House flies don't travel far once they have found a source of food. Their territory may be no larger than your house and back yard. House flies in farming areas might travel as far as several miles to search for fresh manure.

House flies like what we don't like: rotten meat, garbage, spoiled fruit, dying flowers, and animal and human poop. In the country, they love the manure farmers use to fertilize their fields. In your back yard, your compost bin is their salad bar!

House flies don't eat solid food. They suck up what is already liquid. If they find solid food, like something on a plate in the kitchen, they vomit some digestive fluid onto it. This makes part of the food liquid so they can suck it up. Yuck.

House flies have their taste buds in their feet, so they walk on things to find out if it's something that might be good to eat. The buzzing around is not the worst thing. House flies live on and eat filthy stuff with lots of germs, and they carry those germs with them. They transmit over 60 serious diseases, including cholera, dysentery, typhoid, leprosy, and salmonella.

The reason house flies can walk on the ceiling or hang on to windows is that they have sticky pads on part of each foot. This lets them land on almost any solid object, at almost any angle. Almost every time a house fly lands, it poops. This is the number one reason to keep them away from the food on your plate!

DRAGONFLIES

Dragonflies are amazing creatures, like colorful flying needles. They look sort of scary, but they can't sting or hurt people. If one lands on your arm it might try to bite you, but its jaws are not strong enough to break your skin.

Dragonfly

There have been dragonflies for at least 300 million years. Some of the ones flying around in the time of the dinosaurs had wingspans of up to two feet! A dragonfly lays its eggs in water. The babies are larvae, or nymphs, and they live in water for as much as a year, eating smaller creatures, including small fish!

When the nymph becomes a dragonfly, it only lives a few weeks. It feeds on smaller insects, like mosquitoes and moths. During this time it finds a mate and then the female lays her eggs to start the next generation.

Dragonfly Nymph

Butterfly Dragonfly

Fish and fogs eat dragonfly larvae; and birds, spiders, and frogs eat adult dragonflies. There are at least 5,000 dragonfly species. A dragonfly does not have sharp vision, but it can see in all directions. Each of its eyes has about 30,000 lenses, so it can detect anything moving near it. Most dragonflies live near the water where they were born. However, some migrate. The globe skinner migrates across the Indian Ocean to and from Africa, a trip of over 11,000 miles!

HONEY BEES

Honeybees are the only insect that creates food that humans eat. People have built hives for bees to live in for thousands of years, because that makes it easier to get some of the bees' honey. Honey bees are essential for pollinating fruit trees and other plants. Here are some sweet facts about them.

Honey Bee

Drone of Bees

Each hive of bees has one queen, many worker bees, and a few drones. Some of the drones fertilize the eggs the queen lays. The queen lives three or four years, and every day lays hundreds or even thousands of eggs. In one day she may lay her body weight in eggs! Worker bees feed and take care of her so she can go on laying.

The worker bees can fly up to 15 miles an hour, and they usually travel as much as three miles in search of nectar which will be food for the hive. When a bee finds a good food source, it returns to the hive and does a little dance to share the good news. The dance tells other workers which direction to fly in, and how far away the food source is.

Beekeepers with Beehives

Honey bees sting to defend the hive. They can only sting once, and they die when they do it, so it is a huge sacrifice for the good of the queen and the rest of the bees.

To make a pound of honey, bees must bring food from over two million flowers, traveling over 50,000 miles between the flowers and the hive. Any one honey bee only produces a little bit of honey, but an average hive creates as much as four hundred pounds of honey each year.

Beekeepers with Beehives

The bees aren't making that honey for us! They are building up food supplies during the summer so the hive can survive during the winter. Honey is the only food that has every substance needed to support life. And honey never spoils!

HORSEFLIES

There are over three thousand species of horseflies, and they are among the largest species of flies. They live all around the world, except in the Arctic and Antarctic regions.

Horsefly

Horsefly

Just in North America there are over 350 different types of horsefly. Almost all of them will happily bite you, though! Horseflies can be more than an inch long.

Horseflies cut a hole in your skin when they bite you, using jaws that work like saw-toothed scissors. This is why their bite hurts so much. The horsefly then soaks up blood from your wound. If a horsefly bites you, it's a female. Male horseflies eat pollen and nectar because they don't have the sharp biting tools the females have.

Female horseflies need blood from mammals so they can develop their eggs. They then lay the eggs on plants in watery areas. The eggs hatch into larvae which spend a year or two in water or moist ground before they change into horseflies and start flying and biting.

If you are a runner and don't want horseflies to bother you, run in the cooler parts of the day, or on windy days. Some people attach a pin in the shape of a dragonfly to the hats they wear when running, because horseflies are afraid of dragonflies.

Black Horse Fly

A LIVING EARTH

Some insects leave us alone, some insects make food we can eat, and some insects want us to be their food. But all insects are part of the complex chain of life on earth. We may hate the bites of female horseflies, for instance, but male horseflies help pollinate plants. Life is complicated!

Learn more about the creatures we share this Earth with in Baby Professor books like Who Likes Bugs? We Do! And How do Animals Help the Forest Grow?

Visit
BABY PROFESSOR
EDUCATION KIDS
www.BabyProfessorBooks.com
to download Free Baby Professor eBooks
and view our catalog of new and exciting
Children's Books

www.ingramcontent.com/pod-product-compliance
Lightning Source LLC
Chambersburg PA
CBHW060614120726
48002CB00010B/2959